This book is dedicated to the dreamers

The ones who stare out the window and dream about space.
The ones who doodle in their notebooks and dream about characters.
The ones who take apart alarm clocks and dream about robots.
The ones who see a problem and dream of solutions.
The ones who dream of a world better than today.
The ones who dream of equality for all of their friends.
The ones who dream of all the possibilities that lie ahead.
You will be amazing—just go out and do it.

Scott—thank you for dreaming with me and making this possible.
Grammie—thank you for making it possible to dream (and write).
Carrie—There are not enough thank you's in the world for all you have done as my "big sister".
My 3 families—You are big and you are loud and you are the reason I am who I am today.
Ronnie—thank you for being the dream I have been waiting for.
Natalie—thank you for your love of reading and giving me the idea for this dream.
Rehma, Emery, Anthony, Ryder, Walker, and future babies—I hope all of your dreams come true and that this book helps you find those dreams.

All *Dream It & Do It* research was done using only autobiographical materials. Please see the bibliography at www.dreamitandoit.com/bibliography. Role models were chosen that represent the rainbow of children in the world and those that had autobiographical materials available. All due diligence was used to provide only the most accurate information about the job itself and the role model used to highlight the job, however, if you believe there is a detail that deserves further attention, please reach the author at **dreamitanddoitbooks@gmail.com.**

Dream It & Do It – Kid Role Models is launching in the spring of 2021. If you know a child who would be a good role model, share their story on Instagram or Facebook with #dreamit&doit. For updates on this book launch, follow us or join our mail list at **www.dreamitandoit.com.**

FIRST EDITION

Story Numbers

Lemonade Stand (Business)

1. Melissa Butler started the "lemonade stand" (entrepreneur)
2. Ursula Burns runs the "lemonade stand" (CEO)
3. Regina Hartley hires and helps the workers (human resources)
4. Warren Buffet provides money (investor)
5. Mercedes Gonzalez finds the ingredients (buyer)
6. Esther Ndichu gets the ingredients to the "stand" (logistics)
7. Mary Kay sells the "lemonade" (sales)
8. David Kelley learns about who is drinking the "lemonade" (research)
9. Shonda Rhimes runs the project (producer)
10. James Orsulak makes the "lemonade" (manufacturing)
11. J. Alexander teaches how to make the best "lemonade" (consultant)
12. Brandon Rochon gets people to recognize your "lemonade" (advertising)
13. Arian Simone gets people talking about the "lemonade" (public relations)
14. Marcus Collins spreads the word about the "lemonade" (social media mktg)
15. Gianna Gaudini plans parties that serve "lemonade "(event planner)
16. Tim Harford studies how the "lemonade" is bought and sold (economist)

Product Developers

17. Joy Mangano creates new products (inventor)
18. Jonathan and Drew Scott create homes (builder)
19. Hannah Herbst creates robots (electrical engineer)
20. Elon Musk creates cars, rockets and trains (industrial engineer)
21. Maya Penn creates earth friendly products (sustainability)
22. I.M. Pei creates buildings (architect)
23. Majd Mashharawi creates materials (material engineer)
24. Ed McMillen and Tommy Refenes create video games (software developer)
25. Michael Reitz creates roller coasters (mechanical engineer)
26. Kwame Onwuachi creates meals (chef)
27. Jasmine Cho creates baked goods (baker)
28. Jessica Mah creates websites (website developer)
29. Richard Browning creates flying machines (aeronautics engineer)
30. Paul Teutul Jr. creates motorcycles (welder)
31. Alton Brown creates new foods (food scientist)

By Holly A. Sharp

Dear Dreamers,

What an exciting time to be looking to the future. The world around you is changing faster than it did for your parents or your grandparents. Technology is changing every day, the earth is counting on you, and we are working to be a kinder, more equal human race. You will have a major part in all of that. The question is: what will be your role in this change?

Although these people may have different job titles, they have a few things in common:

1. They didn't just dream about doing something. **They did something about it.**
2. **They didn't wait** until they were a "grownup" to start. They found something they were good at or cared about when they were young and followed it.
3. **They kept going when things were hard**. Many people in this book didn't have easy childhoods or were told they were too different to be successful. They didn't care and let their dreams and hard work lead the way.
4. **They weren't scared of failing**. To do something great means trying. Trying means possibly failing. You may try 99 times and fail, but what if you change the world the 100th time you try?
5. **They cared about the world around them**. It's okay to want to make money. It's okay to want to be famous. It's okay to want to follow a talent you're good at. All of these things just get better when you use your money and talents to improve the world around you as well.

I hope that even just one of these stories makes you curious enough to go out and try something new, explore a talent, or learn more. Each and every one of you has nothing but the future ahead of you and every possibility still remains open, even beyond the 100 in this book. Take advantage of this freedom and explore. Try as much as you can, don't be afraid to fail, and when you find something you love or something you care about, keep doing it.

I would love to hear from you, on social media or by email, about what dreams you have and if you found one in this book.

No matter what, keep dreaming and keep doing.

Holly A. Sharp—author, mother, entrepreneur, brand wizard, inventor, and researcher.

"Lemonade Stand"
THE PRODUCTS WE USE AND THE PEOPLE WHO MAKE THEM

Any dream can become a business if you understand all the parts of a "lemonade stand". The most common example used when talking about the business world is the creation of a lemonade stand. It's often the first business that young people run. You meet the different types of people required to start or run a business.

Using the lemonade stand example:
- Starting a lemonade stand makes you an Entrepreneur
- Running a lemonade stand makes you a CEO
- Hiring the workers is human resources
- Providing the money to start the stand is investing
- Gathering the ingredients is purchasing
- Getting the ingredients to the stand is logistics
- Selling the lemonade is sales
- Learning about the people who drink the lemonade is research
- Bringing all the parts together is project management
- Making the lemonade is manufacturing
- Teaching how to make the best lemonade is consulting
- Spreading the word about your stand is advertising and public relations
- Throwing parties that use lemonade is event planning
- Studying how the "lemonade" is bought and sold is done by an economist

You'll also learn about the people who make products. Lots of different skills are required to bring a product to life. These careers require a blend of math, science, and art skills. Each of these product makers has a different blend of these talents, from inventing the product itself to welding it together.

Just like the lemonade stand example, you'll see that many of these people started their own companies when they were young, and you can too. Most just started with a simple idea, a small plan, and a good first step.

Dream about your business and then do it!

Dream of Starting a Company

LIKE

Melissa Butler

Have you ever had an idea so good that you can't believe anybody hasn't thought of it? The truth is, probably lots of people have had an idea similar to yours (or maybe not!). While anyone can have an idea, bringing that idea to life is what is hard. You may agree that selling lemonade on hot day is a good idea, but starting a lemonade stand takes work. After all, you are the one in charge of getting all parts of the business started from scratch. For many people, being your own boss is worth the effort. Melissa Butler had an idea for a product. What started as a project in her kitchen can now be found on Target's shelves!

It all started with a simple question: *How do you know what it means to be beautiful?*

As Melissa flipped through the pages of her fashion magazine, she thought to herself, "None of these women look like me. They all seem to wear their makeup the same way and have the same look. Is this how women of color are supposed to understand what it means to be beautiful? In the pages of magazines?"

She threw her magazine in the trash, convinced that she could do more for beauty than the pictures she was seeing. People should feel free to express themselves and have freedom to be themselves. She started experimenting with her makeup, but was surprised how few products were designed for Black women. Likewise, it took many chemicals to make products that go on your lips and face.

She threw her makeup in the trash, convinced that she could do more for beauty than the makeup she was buying. She bought the ingredients she needed to make the natural makeup she wanted to wear and started making it in her kitchen.

When she was trying to decide what colors to make, she wanted colors that complimented her complexion. Melissa says, "My lipstick became more than just lipstick. I wanted little brown girls to grow up having representation, knowing that they don't have to conform to society's standards of beauty. I want them to be so comfortable in their own skin that they own it."

She says that she's not in the business of simply making makeup. Her Lip Bar business is really about creating products that help people be their most confident selves.

"I am a minimalist girl who believes that a pop of color on the lips will give you enough confidence to take on the day and kick its butt! You are beautiful just the way you are. You don't have to transform to look like the next 'it' girl."

Melissa focuses on helping Black women feel confident through makeup. This unique approach led to her products being sold at Target. Lip Bar was the first product to be sold at Target that was started as a brand-new company. Now, Melissa has her own store in Detroit, MI!

If you have an idea, don't worry about how hard it could be to start a business. Start small like Melissa. She made lipsticks in her kitchen and sold them to her friends until it kept growing and growing.

What can you do to start small with your own idea? If you don't have an idea, but love the idea of working for yourself, go into a store in your community. See if you can talk to the owner. They almost certainly would be interested in talking to you about their work and why they like working for themselves. They might even let you follow them around for the day to learn more!

Dream of Running a Company

LIKE

Ursula Burns

When you play with your group of friends, are you the one that naturally comes up with the plan or takes charge? Maybe you have what it takes to be a CEO. A CEO, chief executive officer, is a professional leader and the head of a company. To be a CEO, you didn't have to start the company in order to lead it. Many companies, like the one for which Ursula Burns worked, did not have a single owner. So, they needed to hire someone to become the single leader.

Burns grew up in a poor part of New York City. Her mom had to work hard to give her opportunity. Being grateful to her mother, she says, "I had a mother who would stress that how my life started would not be a reflection of how my life would turn out. It was about how hard I work and how much confidence I have."

She began her career as an "accidental engineer." In fact, Ursula didn't consider engineering as an option until it was presented to her. She'd taken a test that helps students determine where they are skilled. Then, a counselor at her school called her into their office and said, "Ursula, look at this score. You seem to have what it takes to be a good engineer." Ursula She took this to heart, studied and became more than a good engineer. She was a great engineer.

Ursula started her career as a summer intern at a company called Xerox, who made copy machines. Summer internships are a way for college students to get experience while they are studying. This same company where she had the most entry-level job is the same company where she would become the leader.

Eight years after being hired, there were a lot of people talking together. The topic of diversity came up, and Ursula Burns stood up to share a different opinion than everyone else. Her opinion wasn't popular, and as a result, she thought she would lose her job. Instead, another leader in the company saw this and respected her bravery. After getting to know her better, he asked her to be his assistant. Again, she did something that wasn't popular and said, "Why would I want to be someone's assistant?"

He convinced her, however, to take the job. Today, she says it is one of the most important jobs she ever took. Because of this "assistant" job, she got to see a lot of the leaders of the company, how leadership worked and knew with confidence that, "Yeah, I can do this too."

It would take another nineteen years of doing lots of different jobs, but in 2009, Ursula took over as the first African American leader to run a company of this size. She didn't let this intimidate her. She says, "I found it very normal to be 'the only.' I think that, instead of seeing it being a burden, I saw it as an opportunity. It gave me the chance to stand out."

During her time as CEO, she made some big and bold decisions. She believes that, "Leadership is about taking a stand. You can't just babysit a business." She proved that, if you work hard and believe in yourself, it doesn't matter where you come from. You can still "make it to the top."

If being a leader is a challenge you think you can take on, Junior Achievement is a great place to start. It is an organization that helps kids of all ages get excited about business and leadership. Find out if your school participates in the program. If your school does not participate, a great way to show leadership is to figure out what it would take to bring the program to your school!

Dream of Hiring People

LIKE

Regina Hartley

When you try out for the school play or to be on the basketball team, someone has to make the decision of who is the best person to cast or to play. The same thing happens when you're looking for a job.

The person helping to decide who gets the job has the title of "human resources." Often there are a lot of people who apply for a job, so this person can sometimes have a hard time choosing. Regina Hartley believes that, upon hiring people, we should consider people who are "scrappy!"

Regina describes one scrappy person she met. This man had been given up for adoption. He never finished college, he had lots of different odd jobs, he spent a year living in India and he had a disorder that makes reading difficult (called dyslexia). She wondered, "Would you hire this person?" Well, it turned out that this person was named Steve Jobs. He was Apple's creator. In fact, Jobs was responsible for all the Macs, iPhones and iPads in the world.

Regina says that "scrappy" people are good at overcoming challenges.

These are people who have had hard things happen to them when they were young or didn't have it easy growing up. When things get tough, people who have had to overcome more than most have proven that they won't quit.

One man she hired was living in China many years ago. He was forced to leave his home, work as a farmer and give up his schooling. One day, he learned that there was a test he could take to get a high school degree. Though, he had to take it in three months. He studied after work every night for three months straight to learn everything he was supposed to learn in junior high and high school.

Today, this man has gone to college (twice), has a great job, and both of his children have college degrees. He was able to follow his dreams because someone in human resources took the time to see him as a "scrapper," instead of someone with an inferior type of high school degree.

Regina knows what it is like to be scrappy, because she herself was born into a difficult home. Her father was sick and unable to help care for the family, leaving her mother to raise five children on her own. They didn't have a place to live sometimes, and when they did, they never had a car, a phone or a washing machine. She had to take lots of different jobs to help pay for her own school, but someone took a chance on her. Now, she is the one in charge of hiring lots of other people.

Human resource people also do other types of jobs to help support workers once they are hired as well.

If you want to understand all the different jobs you could get (besides reading this book!), one fun thing you can do is to ask a grownup to help you look at their LinkedIn website. You can search for jobs based on hobbies you have like: basketball, cooking, or video games. See what comes up. You can also put in titles of jobs that you found in this book to see what type of companies are hiring for those jobs. Read the descriptions and look at different people who work at those companies. (Some might know your parents). Go to the company website. You will see that there are a lot of jobs and a lot of people hiring for them.

Dream of Helping Companies Grow

LIKE

Warren Buffet

Do you ever have fundraisers at your school where you sell candy bars to raise money? You buy that candy from the store for $0.10. If you sell that same piece of candy to your grandma for $0.25, you earned $0.15 for your fundraiser. This is what investors do. They find companies that are worth one amount and then give them money to grow and sell them at a higher amount. Warren Buffet started as a normal kid from a normal town with normal parents. After a life of investing in companies and helping them grow, he is one of the richest people in the whole world.

Being able to identify companies that have the potential to be worth more tomorrow than they are today requires being good with numbers. This trait was very true of Warren when he was young. He has had a love of numbers for as long as he could remember. He was always playing around with them. His aunt bought him a *World Almanac* as a gift, which is a book with all sorts of number-based facts about the world. It was one of his favorite gifts. Over fifty years later, he still knows that, "in 1930, the population of his hometown, Omaha, Nebraska was 214,006!"

As his love for numbers grew, he wanted to do more than just memorize fun facts. He went to his local library and took out a book called, *1,000 Ways to Make $1,000*. This inspired him to find lots of different ways to take something that had one price and figure out how to make it worth a higher price. He put old pinball machines in barbershops and split the earnings with the barbershop owner. He bought cans of Coca-Cola and sold them on hot days for a penny more than he bought them. He started a paper route where he could also sell magazines, and he invested in farm land and split the profits with the farmer and sold stray golf balls back to the golfers. By the time he graduated high school, he had made as much as some grownups make in a year. He was so convinced in his ability to figure out how to make money that he told his sister, "I will be a millionaire by the time I am thirty."

After college, he invested in his first company, which meant he owned part of the company. He compared his investment to hitting a baseball. If baseball players didn't have to worry about strikes, they would hit a lot more balls because they would only swing at the pitches they knew they could hit. This is what finding companies to invest in should be like. He says, "The trick is to wait for the pitch and to swing at the balls right in your strike zone. Don't let people tell you when to swing." What he means is that he takes his time and finds companies he thinks are the right ones to buy, even if it takes a while to find them. You may recognize some of the companies that Warren has invested in – Coca-Cola, DQ ice cream and Fruit of the Loom.

The truly wonderful thing about Warren Buffet as an investor is that he doesn't just buy and sell things for the sake of making money- he does it to make the world a better place. Of the billions of dollars that he has made, he has promised to give ninety-nine percent back to the world to help make it better. Each of his three children also run their own "do-good" company and continue the legacy of their father.

If you are interested in investing and figuring out how to buy and sell things in order to create value – you should try selling something, like Warren did when he was young. It can be as simple as a lemonade stand, or maybe there is an art or craft you are good at that you can sell. There are lots of ideas in books, like the one Warren read, to get you started as well. Maybe your parents have things they'd like to get rid of. Have a yard sale and see if you can make some money…maybe even put some aside for charity.

Dream of Buying Things

LIKE

Mercedes Gonzalez

Do you get a thrill from going to the store? Do you like seeing the new products on the shelf? Do you like hunting for just the right purchase? Being a buyer is shopping for a living, but with someone else as a customer. When you go to Target to shop for back to school clothes, a buyer makes the choices for what Target sells to you. It's the job of someone like Mercedes Gonzalez, a clothing buyer, to understand your fashion choices. So well, in fact, that they know you will want to purchase a Mickey Mouse jacket this year and a jean jacket next year. Being a buyer isn't limited to clothing. Someone buys all the parts for your car to make it into a usable vehicle. Meanwhile, someone buys all the groceries in the grocery store and there's someone looking for toys around the world who decides which ones should fill your favorite toy store.

Understanding what to buy was something Mercedes learned early in life. As a child, she was allowed to work in her uncle's dress shop and help him with all sorts of tasks. Even at the age of thirteen, she was allowed to try new things and learn from her mistakes. Sometimes she even fixed the mistakes that her uncle made! After college, she was unable to find the job she wanted. So, she returned to his dress shop while continuing her job hunt. Soon, she saw an opportunity to sell his dresses in larger stores, but she would need to buy more material and at cheaper prices. When Mercedes approached her uncle with the idea of buying their dresses from people who could make lots of them and for less money, he was skeptical, but agreed to try.

When she arrived in the city where her dresses might be made, she found a big building that sold different products on every floor. A floor for toys, a floor for electronics, a floor for home goods, a floor for bikes – they seemed to sell everything. They even sold the exact dress that her uncle has been making for years. She was able to buy the same dress for three dollars that her uncle was making for twelve dollars. This allowed her uncle to sell his dress in Wal-Mart and reach many more women with his design.

Being a buyer, however, isn't always about getting the lowest price. After helping her uncle, she was hired to buy clothing for lots of different people. She learned that understanding the person wearing the clothing was more important than creating a bargain. A buyer needs to buy the right things and sell them in the right way.

Mercedes would help teach this lesson to other people. In her work, a man who had beautiful boots that he wanted to sell in New York City approached her for help. The boots cost almost $1,000. He bought a store in the middle of the busiest intersection in the city – Times Square. "I am so lucky," he told her, "I have found this great location. Now, all I have to do is sell thirty pairs per day!" She tried to convince him that Times Square was for tourists who want to eat or see a show, rather than for rich people in New York, who were ready to spend their money on an expensive purchase. When he wouldn't listen, she made him stand in front of his store for half an hour and count the shopping bags. She was right. They saw two bags, one for an "I love New York" t-shirt and one from the M&M store. Being good at buying things is actually about being good at knowing what will sell.

One fun way to practice this is to help with the family grocery shopping. This way, you can practice buying things for someone that isn't yourself. Get the budget from your parents, just as Mercedes did from her uncle. Plan out all the food you need for the week. Then, use a grocery-shopping app or go to the store and keep track of your costs. Using this method, be sure you stay on budget. You can't, however, just buy the cheapest items; you have to think about brands and types of foods that the members of your family like. After you finish, you could create a short survey to find out how they felt about your choices.

Dream of Managing Resources

LIKE

Esther Ndichu

The next time you pull through McDonald's, be grateful to the logistics manager of the company for your food being fresh and in stock. It's the job of the logistics manager to get all the parts of your meal from a farm somewhere to your hand.

Let's look at the french fry. McDonald's sells millions of french fries every year. So, they have to get millions of potatoes from lots of different farms to the place where they get chopped up. Then, the chopped-up potatoes go into a truck and are sent to all the different restaurants. Finally, they are fried and sold to you for less than a dollar. Understanding how food moves from once place to another was part of Esther Ndichu's job at UPS. She was the humanitarian supply chain director and was responsible for getting food to people in areas where it is hard to get.

Esther was born on a farm in Kenya. Many people she knew were farmers, including her own family. Even as a child, she could remember food going to waste because it would spoil before it was sold. This happened because they had a hard time getting extra food to the local market to sell. She recalls watching her uncle feed the extra food to the cows, instead of being able to sell it and use the money. How is it possible to live in a place with so much good land and rainfall, but still have food go to waste and people go hungry? As an adult, she would learn that this waste was a really big deal.

She learned that there are 800 million people in the world that go hungry (that is almost three times the number of people in the United States). What surprised her even more than the number of hungry people was that there was enough food in the world being produced to feed these hungry people. The problem is that food is being wasted, just like she saw on her uncle's farm. In fact, she says that one-third of all the food produced in the world ends up going to waste.

She realized – this is not a food shortage problem. This is a logistics problem.

The reason it is a logistics problem is because the food to feed people is not ending up in the right locations at the right time. Similar to the McDonald's french fry example, if enough potatoes are grown to make all the needed french fries, but McDonald's runs out of french fries, it's the problem of getting the potatoes to where they needed to be – not the number of potatoes.

And so, Esther is helping to solve this issue with logistic solutions.

One reason that her uncle and many other farmers throw out good food is because they can't get it to a local market to sell. The market is either too far away or they can only sell what they can carry.

This is the perfect problem for a logistics person to solve. This simply means that a better vehicle is in order – and that's what she did. In the Democratic Republic of Congo, the farmers were given "cargo bikes" to bring all their extra food to the market. This allowed them to make money to buy other foods from other farmers – and maybe even more bikes!

There are lots of other examples of how logistics can help solve the problem of wasted food around the world. However, Esther believes that if we work to solve them one by one, through logistics, that not one person needs to go hungry.

If you are interested in learning more about this topic, there is a show called, "Where It Comes From." At the time of this writing, it was available on Amazon Prime. It's all about the products we use every day and what they have to go through to reach us.

Dream of Selling Products

LIKE

Mary Kay Ash

Before the backpack was invented, kids would bind their books together with a leather strap and carry them back and forth to school. Books would fall out, either getting dirty or damaged. When someone was selling the first backpack, the skill was showing how it would solve the problem of damaging schoolbooks, not just a cool new bag with straps. A sales person is someone who helps you understand a product so that you will buy it. What makes a great salesperson is that they understand solving problems, and not just selling products. No one understood this better than Mary Kay Ash, the woman who created a new way of selling makeup.

Mary Kay was forced to gain confidence at a young age, doing things that most kids don't learn to do until they are living on their own. Her father was sick when she was growing up. Consequently, her mother worked long hours to support the family, which left Mary Kay to take care of her father. At the age of seven, she was cooking dinners and taking the bus by herself into the city to go shopping. Mary Kay is grateful for this challenging time in her life. "You can do it" were words she heard from her mother over a thousand times when she would trust her with grownup duties. "Whether my mom really knew if I could or not, who knows, but it made me believe that I could," she said. It is this confidence, from her Mom, that served her through her life. Without it, Mary Kay Cosmetics might have fizzled before it even began.

When she was old enough to have kids of her own, Mary Kay was responsible for providing for her family the way her mother was. Because of her warm personality, she was good at listening to people and selling them things they really needed. She quickly became a top salesperson for a company that made home goods. She would not only sell products, but she would also train other salespeople, mostly men, on how to sell. One day, she heard that a man she had trained was being paid more than she was and thought to herself, "Well, this isn't fair!"

Frustrated by the fact that she was treated differently as a woman, she decided to write a book about the challenges she faced, in hopes of helping others like her. Mary Kay put all her thoughts down on paper and realized she had more than just a book. She had an idea for a business. "I wanted a company where everyone was treated fairly and equally, with honesty and integrity. I want it to be a company where everyone applied the golden rule – because it's the greatest rule in the whole world." The golden rule says that you should treat others as you treat yourself. In this way, Mary Kay wanted to give women the potential to earn as much as they were worth regardless of their background or experience.

Her idea for how products should be sold involved making it as easy as possible to listen for problems that needed to be solved. Her idea was to sit a group of women around a table. Their makeup would be off, and they would get to ask lots of questions. "How do I get my skin to be smoother?" "What do I do about this red patch on my nose?" "Should I be wearing reds or pinks on my lips?" The more questions these women asked, the more excited they would get about the products being sold.

There is no talk of pricing or order taking. These women feel comfortable trying out different looks because they are at home, seated next to their friends and comfortable asking personal questions. At the end of the night, the women excitedly purchase the makeup that best solves the problem they are having and everyone, including the saleswoman, leaves happy. Today, this is more than an idea. Over two million people around the world sell Mary Kay. None of it is sold in stores and it is always shown with friends at home. This is one of the biggest makeup companies in the world because Mary Kay understood sales. Do not think about "How much can I sell you today?" She says to think about, "What can I do to help you feel better about yourself?"

You shouldn't be scared of sales because you have to "sell" something. If you find a good product, selling is more like making new friends every day. It involves figuring out how to make their life easier or better. What problems do you see in your neighborhood that sales could help fix? Is there a park with people who might be thirsty? Do you notice a lot of dirty cars when it hasn't rained in a while? Do your neighbors need their paths cleared of snow or weeds? Is there a holiday coming up where people might want decorations for their front door? Think about a problem people have and I bet you will find an idea just waiting for you to go sell!

Dream of Learning About People

LIKE

David Kelley

Did you know that you're more likely to buy something you wouldn't normally buy if you are standing around and waiting? Imagine that you are in line for a long roller coaster ride and it's hot and sunny. You're more likely to buy an ice cream, and for more money, while you are in line than when you're walking around. One Girl Scout realized this, and so, her troop set up a booth selling cookies at a popular oil change location. They sold ten times more than ever before because they understood this principle of "bored purchasing." Learning about how people think when it comes to buying and using products is a job called consumer research. By understanding more about the people who are buying our products (like the Girl Scout did), we can do a better job of making and selling them. David Kelley is responsible for creating an entire company who's celebrated for learning about people.

David often thinks about a moment in his childhood when a classmate was building a clay horse. Another student commented that the horse was not very good. So, the boy who created the horse crumpled his clay up and put it back in the pile, deflated at his ability to be creative. This made young David wonder why some people could be creative while others couldn't. Many adults have this perspective as well. You're either a creative person who likes art and design or you are a technical person that loves math and science.

It's this blend of being creative and technical that Kelley uses to learn about people and the products they use.

He and his team were interviewed by a popular news show. They wanted to show off how the combination of creative thinking and technical know-how could work. So, they completely redesigned a shopping cart in twenty-four hours. Before they came up with one single idea, they had to learn about the people who used the shopping cart.

First, they spoke with people who worked at the stores. From this group they learned about people stealing the carts and that they were difficult to move around. Then, they talked to moms who would put their children in the carts. They further learned about problems with safety and children having something to play with. They finally talked to people who went shopping a lot, while watching them shop and looking at some of the troubles there were having. They were bumping into other people and they were stacking heavy items on top of light items. Finally, they watched the person as they unpacked their groceries at home. By doing this, they saw that they were all disorganized. The groceries took longer to put away because they were not unpacking similar things together. You can see below the new cart that the team designed by applying the learning with creative thinking and technical skills. Had they just sat around and thought of ideas, the cart wouldn't have been nearly as good. In retrospect, they wouldn't have learned from the actual people who used it.

David Kelley loved this way of learning about people so much that he started a a business called IDEO, that focused entirely on helping other companies learn more about the people for whom they made products. They hired all sorts of people, which included doctors, artists, designers and business people; because David believed that all people could learn this process and think creatively. Today, his company has developed insights that led to new medical devices, smart clothing, educational programs, electronics and many more things.

A great way to learn more about this type of thinking is to learn about the products that resulted from the process. Go to YouTube and search for "design thinking" or "human centric design" examples. There you should find some fun videos to inspire you to think about a career in consumer-based research. You can even find the "IDEO shopping cart" example if you search for it.

Dream of Producing a Product

LIKE

Shonda Rhimes

When your family plans out a vacation, someone is acting like the family project manager. It's the job of a project manager to oversee all the moving parts of a project. For your family vacation, this means planning out everything you will do or where you will stay with the money that you have available. It means making sure that you have reservations and tickets purchased with enough time that things are not sold out. It might also mean finding people needed to accomplish the things you want to do like hiring a tour guide or bus driver. Project managers work with all sorts of teams to make sure they have the money, the time and the people they need to accomplish their goal. In Hollywood when you oversee the making of an entire show, this is called producing. Shonda Rhimes produces TV shows.

At her core, Shonda is a writer; however, she also produces the TV shows that she writes. When Shonda was a child, she loved making up stories. Shonda was telling stories before she even knew how to write. She would tell her stories into a tape recorder and beg her mother to type them up for her. She would tell stories to her classmates as well. She made up a story about her mom being a Russian spy, and that her mom had to flee the country. Now, they are never allowed back. "The same love of story telling tales took me from having to repeat the rosary (when I was caught) all the way to Hollywood," says Shonda.

The first TV show that she wrote was about a group of Doctors called *Grey's Anatomy*. However, this show was different from other shows because she included all sorts of different people that other shows often overlook. "I made a show with people that looked the way that the world looked and gave them real lives,"Shonda says.

Shonda created a company called Shondaland. Through this company, she was more than just a brilliant writer. She was also the producer (project manager) in charge of making sure that each episode was made correctly, on time and on budget. She got to choose whom the actors were within her shows. She further got to choose the things that would happen to the characters on the show.

When it came time to end their sixteenth season, Shonda wanted it to be really special as it was an important moment for the lead characters. In fact, she chose how the ending would be filmed and even the song that would be used to convey the strength and friendship between the two female doctors on the show.

Being a project manager means being comfortable making decisions, being organized and taking action. Shonda would say that project managers should, "Ditch dreaming and start doing. Dreams don't just come true because you dream them. They come true because you do them."

She also tells young people that, no matter what career you choose, "If you are a kid and you are out there and chubby, nerdy, not cute, shy, invisible or in pain, whatever your race, gender or orientation - you are not alone. Your tribe of people is out there waiting for you."

If managing projects sounds fun to you, see if you can help with your next family vacation. Plan out the where, the how, the when and the budget to do it. As Shonda Rhimes learned, you get more of a say in what happens when you are the one overseeing the process!

Dream of Building Products in Space

LIKE

James Orsulak

What's the most important part of the lemonade stand? The lemonade! To make lemonade, you have to squeeze the lemons, add the sugar, add the water, and stir. You could easily do these steps by hand for one glass of lemonade. However, to make one hundred glasses of lemonade, you might need a faster process. This faster process is called manufacturing.

Manufacturing uses a combination of human and robot power to assemble all the pieces of the products we use. If you like the idea of working with robots, manufacturing uses hundreds of robots to make the things we use and buy every day. One of the challenges of manufacturing is that it takes up lots of space and can contribute to pollution. James Orsulak thinks that he has a solution for this—manufacturing in space.

James hopes that if you want to work in manufacturing in the next one hundred years that it means that you must also want to live in space. His dream is to create floating manufacturing plants that orbit the earth, make all of the things we need, send the finished products back to earth, but leave behind the pollution that manufacturing causes.

James thinks we could start by manufacturing products that create energy. Energy production is very hard on our planet. We mine for coal and metals. We drill for oil and natural gas. What if we could do that in space instead? We could build a solar farm where the sun shines for 24 hours a day and send the harnessed energy back to earth. James says, "This technology already exists, but it is too expensive to build it on earth and bring it to space. We have to manufacture it in space."

James says that outer space is full of all the raw materials that we need to make tons of different products. James once worked for a company that would drill asteroids that were near the earth, looking for these materials that we could bring back and use. But James wants to know, "What if we kept those materials in space and used them for manufacturing?"

Another one of his ideas for space manufacturing is making cellphones. Believe it or not, cell phones are made of raw materials from the earth. James points out that, "The most expensive component in your phone is called platinum and when we manufacture our phones from materials here on earth, we create emissions and toxic chemicals that are a byproduct of manufacturing. However, platinum is readily available in near-earth asteroids passing by us all the time." What if humans and robots in outer space could make your cell phone?

James knows that sometimes the question gets asked, "Why should we be spending so much time exploring space, when there are so many problems here on earth?" James believes that the answer your generation should be responding with is that space may actually be the answer.

If you're interested in manufacturing, you may have to study the ones here on earth first. Go to YouTube and look up your favorite foods or toys followed by "manufacturing process." Some examples you can start with are Crayola and Bomb Pop popsicles.

Dream of Being an Expert

LIKE

J. Alexander

Do you have a hobby that you love and know lots of information about? If so, people who are experts on specific topics can be a consultant. A consultant provides expert advice on a topic that they understand well. So, when someone has a question about a certain topic, they call a consultant to help find the answer. J. Alexander is a consultant for fashion models. He teaches them the proper way to walk up and down the runway.

J. Alexander always loved beautiful clothing. As a child, he rummaged through his mothers' closet, trying on her "going out" clothes because they were so beautiful. When it was time to buy clothes for going back to school, his mom gave him twenty-five dollars to spend on two pairs of pants, two shirts and a pair of shoes. While he was out shopping, he came across the most beautiful pair of shoes he'd ever seen. "I need these much more than I need pants and shirts," he thought. Although, when he returned home, his mother disagreed. She immediately made him go back to the store and return them. However, he wouldn't give up on owning these shoes. He started delivering newspapers, and as soon as he made enough money, J. Alexander returned to the store. He bought the shoes his mother made him return. After he started making money with his paper route and could afford to buy fabrics, he would use his grandmother's sewing machine to duplicate the expensive clothing he saw in magazines. "I can't wait for you to get rich off my old sewing machine," his grandmother would tell him.

And that he did. J. Alexander was always very confident. And, it showed in the way he moved and walked. He would show off his beautiful creations by doing a supermodel walk up and down one of the highest fashion streets in New York. He would stop in front of his favorite stores and pose for the women working there. A manager at one of the nicest shops on the street noticed him and loved the way he dressed and walked. One afternoon, she came rushing out of the store to tell him that a store down the street was looking for people to be in its fashion show. She said, "I've seen you walking up and down the street and you have the perfect walk." He ran as fast as he could to the audition. When it was his turn, he showed off his walk, which he had practiced every day, and got the job!

"My confidence stems from the fact that, as soon as I realized it was possible, I started living my life the way I wanted. I didn't care what people thought of me. From the age of twelve, I hadn't any interest in following the crowd," he says.

His confidence continued to pay off as he began teaching others how to develop better "walks." Once he was a regular model, he would hang out backstage with friends before their shows. He would give friends advice about their walk and how they should carry themselves based on what they were wearing. "Many models understood how to move for a camera, but not the runway." Someone saw J. Alexander doing this and said, "You should get paid for this!" He found space for his office and opened his own consulting agency. Models would come to him to improve their runway walk. Eventually, he would travel the world to attend fashion shows and teach models in dozens of different countries.

J. Alexander ended up using his consulting skills to help contestants on a TV show called *Project Runway*. He continues to let his confidence shine and tries to help others do the same. He says, "I see so many people blindly following trends to the point where they all look the same and it breaks my heart. Get creative when it comes to how you present yourself to the world. Fashion is all about the excitement and the unexpected."

It doesn't matter what type of topic you consult on, but all consultants must have confidence in themselves and the topic in which they're experts. Do you have a hobby or talent to which you're dedicated? Use the library or the internet to figure out if there are consultants who work in the industry you care about. What do you need to learn in order to become enough of an expert that one day you can get paid to teach others about your own passion?

Dream of Being a "Chief Creative Officer"

LIKE

Brandon Rochon

When you write your Christmas wish list, how do you choose the toys that will make the final cut? Probably some of the winners are toys your friends play with, but some are probably because of toys that you see on television.

Advertising helps inform us about the products that are for sale that we might be interested in buying. The best advertisements are like stories. They do more than just sell us a product; they move us in some way and make us care about what is being sold.

Creative minds, like those of Brandon Rochon, work to figure out the best story to tell about the brands that we love.

When Brandon was young, he thought that he wanted to be in theater. He loved storytelling and thought he would tell his stories through being an actor. He entertained his school friends by making up stories. He entertained his parents' friends with songs and dances.

He remembers a party that his mother hosted when he was four years old. "I dressed myself up in a little blue suit and cowboy boots and started entertaining people at the party. People loved it and started handing me coins like I was a street performer. My mom told me that I had a gift for storytelling and persuading people to find joy." Brandon continued to develop his storytelling skills. One day, he saw a great ad on television. For those thirty seconds, he was taken in by the story. In that moment, Brandon realized how powerful advertising could be and decided to use his storytelling skills to make more advertising like the one he saw.

As he was growing up, he was okay with being different. "I was an outlier – not an outsider," he says. He liked being different because it made people take notice of him. He may have been different, but he was liked because he was good at bringing people together. He could do this because he took the time to really "see" people and get to know them.

Brandon is recognized as a talented, creative mind because he does not think of what he does as selling products. He sees himself as a cultural expert. He thinks about the people using the product rather than the product itself. "People do not invite brands into their home. They invite people. So, I have to help brands talk like people."

Brandon helped create a brand called SNKR (like sneaker). SNKR tells stories that celebrate sneaker culture. He says, "Every sneaker has a sole. Every soul has a story." He dives into the culture surrounding people who love their shoes, especially their sneakers, and tells their stories. The biggest part of being a chief creative officer (yes, this is a real title) is staying with the times. Knowing what is going on in culture from gaming, fashion, movies, music, sneakers, Tic Tok, comic books, art and celebrities. He uses his understanding of trends and culture to tell a story and getting people excited about your product.

If being a storytelling, culture guru sounds fun to you, then Brandon has some advice: "Lean into the magic of creativity." If people don't understand you because the worlds your mind is making up are so different and so weird, don't let people make you feel like an outsider. What's great about working in advertising is that I get to make up these magical worlds. Create worlds that people didn't know existed until I came up with it, but then they can't live without it. This gift is special. It's a super power."

Dream of Getting People to Talk

LIKE

Arian Simone

Do you know people at your school that seem to know and be friends with everyone? If they have a story to tell at the beginning of recess, by the end of recess everyone knows it. This is the type of person that would be good at public relations. If you think about the phrase "public relations," you'll see that public = people while relations = relationships. So, basically it means having lots of relationships with people. People who work in public relations, like Arian Simone, use these relationships to help spread news. Arian Simone worked for famous actors and singers to help them spread the news about an upcoming movie or concert.

As a child, Arian would win every fundraising competition she entered because she was so good at talking to people. She would open her mother's phone book and call everyone her parents knew, whether she knew them or not. She wasn't afraid to get to know someone new. When she was in high school and before she was legally allowed to work, Arian applied for a job at the mall. No one noticed how young she was because she was winning prizes for selling more than anyone else. For her, it was easy. It was just talking to people and getting to know them.

After college, Arian Simone moved from Detroit, Michigan to Los Angeles, California. There, she chased her dream of working in public relations for famous brands and people. She struggled at first and even had to sell off her clothing to buy groceries. But eventually, her ability to make friends paid off again. She bought a small office that was in the same building as a radio station. One day, while someone was waiting to be interviewed on the radio show, they met her in the hallway. The next thing you know, he was offering to help her get a job on the movie he was making.

It was only a few short years later that Arian would look around her and be grateful to God for all of the great friends she had made in Hollywood. She was helping promote movies for some of the most famous actors and promote concerts for some of the most famous singers. She says that, "Relationships are one of your most valuable resources." She's successful because she works hard to get to know so many people. Therefore, when she has a party to throw or story to tell, lots of people will work to help her tell it.

This applies to projects in her own life as well. She decided that she wanted to start a magazine to tell the "fearless" stories of all the people she was meeting. In her first issue, Arian wanted to feature young women of color who were making their start in movies and television. Another magazine had recently done something similar, but she felt that there were not enough people of color included.

The night before the article was getting ready to go live, she stayed up late thinking of all the people she had met over the years. Arian sent them an email about her magazine article. The next morning when she woke up, famous singers and movie stars were already sharing it. In fact, it was on over 100 different websites and news outlets. All were talking about it. She was all over the internet and she hadn't even had her morning coffee yet!

Being in public relations means making friends with influential and famous people in the media, in Hollywood, and in business. If you think that living in this world sounds fun to you, you should practice keeping up with the relationships you already have. Start an address book with everyone you know. Likewise, collect his or her birthday. Do you have what it takes to remember for one whole year to send birthday cards to everyone you know? If so, maybe you have what it takes to work in PR!

Dream of Making Social Media Friends

LIKE

Marcus Collins

What is the most valuable thing you own? You might say it's an expensive toy or collectors' item. You might say it's your bike or scooter. Marcus Collins would say that it's the people in your life like parents, siblings, or friends. These are the people that we invest all our free time to be with and couldn't replace if they were gone. This is why social media is something that people love so much. It's a way for us to stay connected to the people we care about. Marcus Collins is a social media expert who understands how to use social media in positive ways that bring people (and sometimes products) together.

Even at a young age, Marcus cared about bringing people together. For him, this was done through singing. He attended church with his family and saw how singing made people feel welcome and comfortable with each other. Marcus thought that if he could spend his life making people feel this connected to each other, surely he would have done something right.

Marcus would be the first to admit that he wasn't an "early adopter" of social networking platforms. He wasn't quite sure what it was, but he knew some of his college classmates were joining and he didn't want to be left out. From the moment he joined and started sharing updates and photos with his small group of friends, he knew that this was something special. As his friend group grew and grew, he thought, *If people are having nourishing meaningful relationships because of these technologies, maybe companies could foster meaningful relationships as well.*

After finishing his graduate studies, he set out to try and make this happen. The first company he helped was Apple, launching its very first Facebook campaign. This would be the start of many more to come. He worked with big companies like State Farm, GORE-TEX, McDonald's—even a sandwich shop called Potbelly's. How does a sandwich shop use social media to make friends?

Well, this sandwich shop is well known for the musicians that would play in the store while people were eating. He noticed how the music seemed to make everyone in the shop a little bit happier. He realized, "What if we could do this for people on social media?" Marcus worked with the sandwich shop to find people on Twitter who seemed to be having a bad day. One girl's pet bird died. Another girl fell off her bike. For each person they found, the sandwich shop musicians would write a song just for that person and send it to them on Twitter. It made so many people happy that the sandwich shop was able to make more friends than it ever had before, all without trying to sell a sandwich.

Marcus was right. Companies should try and make friends instead of customers and social media could help them do that. Not long after helping the sandwich shop, a new basketball team was coming to Brooklyn and they needed help getting the neighborhood excited.

Marcus understood how much pride people in Brooklyn have for where they live. He helped create a community of people, including celebrities who grew up there, that loved the idea of a team that was special to their community. By the very first game, the team already had a huge following of loyal fans that banned together to welcome the new team.

Social media will be a big and powerful part of your life, like it or not. Social media is only as good as the people who use it and the ways that they use it. If you have a desire to help keep social media a positive place, focused on creating relationships, you might have a future in social media.

Dream of Planning Events

LIKE

Gianna Gaudini

Think back to your favorite birthday party or maybe one you attended. What made it special? For many, birthday parties are fun because there is a theme that happens throughout the event. The cake, food, decorations, games, and party favors all work together. This is because someone took the time to plan out the event ahead of time and make all of the parts of the event come together. This person is an event planner.

For small events like a birthday party or big events like a wedding or business meeting, an event planner unites all aspects of a celebration. Gianna Gaudini does event planning for companies like Google. She throws some of the biggest events you have ever seen. She says, "I sometimes think I am a "memory weaver" with each event I plan. It can be a dinner at my home or an event for 30,000 people."

Gianna says she never was a dreamer. "I was a go-getter. My whole life, when I fell in love with some wild idea of making something major happen, I would think about all the things it would take to make it a reality."

She began to see how this "go-getter" attitude would make her a great event planner when she started hosting weekly dinners at her home in college. She invited friends over to her college apartment every Wednesday. She created fancy dishes and set the mood with flowers, candles, and music. These dinners became something everyone looked forward to. She worked on dinner as her friends were working on homework. Soon, others asked to be invited. Gianna realized these events were a great way to meet new people and bring people together. The dinners reminded her of dinners she used to plan with her mother. For Christmas dinner, she would set the dining room table with a different theme every year. Often, colorful ornaments adorned each family members name and would serve as festive place settings.

Today, Gianna still hosts elaborate dinner parties. Now, however, she mainly hosts important business people. Her job at these dinners is to create an event that motivates and inspires them to have great ideas. One dinner she hosted was aimed at getting people to work together. So, she decided on an autumn theme and aimed to create a festive, together feeling – like you get at a family Thanksgiving dinner.

She thought about all the possibilities and she chose a location at a ranch, with a farm-like feel. She served farm-fresh foods that are popular in the fall, like pumpkin soup. Each soup was served right inside of a small pumpkin. She served the main meal in big bowls where everyone had to share and serve each other, to create a feeling of family. At the end of the event, there was a cozy campfire where people were able to relax and enjoy a s'mores snack. She said, "When you are sitting at a campfire – you're not thinking about stressful things like work." All of these choices created a special atmosphere that an event planner works to create.

Each event is unique and requires different attention. She has done everything from sending a man into an event with a parachute to maneuvering a self-driving car into the entrance of a fancy hotel. Gianna's advice is to, "Start practicing and pick a small project that requires attention to detail and see it through to the end."

You could reach out to your local community center and help plan a charity event or plan a friend's birthday. At the start of your planning, make a mood board. Print off pictures (Pinterest is a great resource) that reflect your imagination of the event's look and feel. Use this as the starting point for your inspiration! Then, once you have your ideas, write down everything you think you need to do to accomplish your ideas.

Don't just dream it, as Gianna would say. Go do it!

Dream of Being a Money Detective

LIKE

Tim Harford

When you go with your family out for ice cream, a flow of money had to take place in order for you to eat your delicious treat. Someone is paid to raise the cows that make the milk. Someone then turns the milk into ice cream. Someone makes the containers into which the ice cream goes. Someone delivers the ice cream in trucks designed to keep the ice cream cold. Someone bought an ice cream shop to serve the ice cream. Finally, you, the customer, buy the ice cream.

Economists study how all these parts of this "money chain" (or economy) work together and how the amount of ice cream that you want (demand) is impacted by the amount of ice cream which can be made (supply). Economists study the impact of all this movement of money. They gather clues about how people might behave in the future – making them a bit like a detective; a money detective. They use these clues to help businesses and the government make decisions about things like how to price a product, how much of a product to make, where to sell the product, or to whom to sell the product. Tim Harford is a money detective that shares what he learns in a newspaper and books. By doing this, Harford helps everyday people better understand how the economy around us works.

Harford went to college to study a different topic. However, while he was in an economics class, he learned about game theory and it was love at first sight. Game theory is a way to help explain how people make decisions. It's one of the many clues that economists use to help predict how people will behave. An example of a game he studied is called prisoners' dilemma. Imagine that you and a friend get into trouble and are separated. Both of you are asked about what you did. If you tell on the other person, you get to go free. However, if the other person tells on you, they will go free and you get in trouble. If neither of you tell on each other, both of you will go free. But if you both tell on each other, both of you will be punished. Studying how people react to the opportunity to avoid punishment is just one of many clues that help economists understand how people make decisions in life and with their money.

Once Harford saw how much fun he had understanding these games, he could see them applied everywhere. From how traffic jams formed, why there are so many Starbucks and why on-the-go coffee is so expensive. One day while he was grocery shopping, he took note of how the exact same products he saw in another store were more expensive in the store in which he was shopping. He knew that the rules he learned about economics could explain it, but that most people didn't understand that. This made him decide to share his superpower with others. So, he developed the identity of "The Undercover Economist." He would write stories about why things happen and how the flow of money or the way people make decisions impact every day things.

One of the stories he told was about Disney World. One way that companies figure out how to make more money is to charge different people different prices. This might seem unfair, but it is done all the time. Disney World does it by offering people who live in Florida a different price than people who live outside of Florida. They know that people coming on vacation from far away are willing to pay more because they only come a few times in their life. They also know that people who live nearby will come more often if the price is not that high. So, they create a rule that allows this to happen and the economic game of "group pricing" seems to work.

There are not a lot of jobs where you are trusted to predict the future, but this is one of them! A great way to start training your mind to think about how other people make decisions is to learn how to play chess. In fact, chess is one style of game theory. If you find that you love the "thinking ahead" that is required to be good at this game, you might make a great economist.

Dream of Creating Product Inventions

LIKE

Joy Mangano

Product inventors are the worlds best problem solvers. They look at the world and are able to see ideas for things that don't yet exist. How do they do this? Not by inventing ideas in their head, but by finding problems to solve and then creating a solution.

By the age of nine, Joy found all sorts of problems to solve. Her dog was injured, and they couldn't get the bandage to stick to his wound, so she invented one. She wanted a tree house with room for all her friends, so she designed one herself – with seven levels! She wanted a fast way to roast seeds, so she used her toaster and foil to figure out how to make that possible.

As an adult, Joy thinks, "The best thing about little Joy, the inventor, is that she didn't think she had to get it perfect to give it a try." Joy never built a tree house, but that didn't stop her. Joy set the toaster on fire trying to make her seed-toasting invention and just thought, "oops."

Joy believes that you are born with fearless creativity as a child. You have ideas and are not scared to take a chance to bring them to life.

As a kid, if you make mistakes and mess things up, it's okay, because you learn what works and what doesn't.

As we grow older, we lose this carefree creativity and allow our fear of failure or being embarrassed to stop us from trying in the first place. Many adults think we have to be good the first time or it's not worth trying. You don't have to be good at something to get started. Just get started!

Joy never "studied" to be an inventor. She realized that she was good at seeing problems and coming up with ideas. Most of all, she had the guts to bring those ideas to life. The way she says it is: "I don't have a superpower or a talent that someone else doesn't have. I have all the same fears and doubts as other people and am not brilliant. I am really normal. What I do have going for me is that I believe in my ideas and have the courage to act on them."

What made Joy famous was a mop she invented when she was a young mom. She was cleaning up a mess and saw a problem: she didn't like how hard it was to wring the water from her mop. She decided to create a mop that didn't get your hands wet and dirty. Her first version of the mop used a toilet paper roll and things from around her house, proving that your idea does not need to be perfect right away; you just need to take the first step and make something.

A TV channel that does nothing but sell products heard about her mops. She went on TV in front of millions of people and the mop sold out right away! Each time she went on TV, she sold more and more until her business became a huge success. Today, Joy has designed dozens of products for peoples' homes that solve lots of different problems.

If you have an idea on how to solve a problem, Joy believes that, "Good ideas don't have to be huge. Think of the cup holder, someone had the idea to put a hollow space in your car to make it easier to hold a drink. Imagine being in the car without a place to put your drink!"

Joy started making products with materials around her house at the age of nine, and you can do the same – just take the first step and see what happens. Pay attention when someone says, "I wish I had (fill in the blank)."

Looking for more inspiration? Go to kidsthinkdesign.com and find weekly product design challenges. You can even submit your product ideas to be featured on the website!

Dream of Creating Houses

LIKE

Jonathan and Drew Scott

As a child, Jonathan Scott was always trying to fix things around the house, but he didn't always wait for something to break first! This is a common trait among kids who grow up to work with their hands. A tradesperson, which includes being a builder, is someone who develops a skill that requires specific on-the-job training, like construction workers, plumbers, electricians, carpenters, and other types of professionals who help build and repair buildings.

Jonathan and Drew Scott are identical twins with their own home-repair show called *Property Brothers*. In this show, they find old homes for other people and fix them up. Each episode, the brothers buy a house and work together to make it like new. This skill came from growing up on a farm where both brothers learned to build and repair things.

When they were just seven years old, their Dad gave them a challenge to build something that would make money. The boys, a bit surprised, looked at each other, but their Dad said, "You are never too young to start. If you are told you are too young or inexperienced, go out and find five ways to prove that person wrong."

When looking at the newspaper one day, the boys could not believe their luck. They saw an ad that described a job they could do together.

"Calling all clowns. Entertain at parties and parades. Attend Saturday clown school and earn your clown degree."

They became professional clowns and were very good at it. Being twins made them unique and they were both comfortable performing in front of people. People loved them so much, they realized, "We have enough of a fan base to branch out on our own and make more money!" At the age of ten, they were earning thousands of dollars being clowns and had their first taste of how much they loved performing.

Because of this love of performing, Jonathan worked to become a magician and invested in shows and props. Drew played college sports and dreamed of being a professional athlete or an actor. Both of them loved the spotlight and were working on increasing the fame they found as clowns.

When they got to college, they were excited to start their careers. However, they needed money to fuel their dreams of being famous. Because of the building skills they had learned on the farm, home construction was a good choice as a side job. To make money, they would buy houses, make them better, and sell them. It turned out that this skill would actually be the one to make them famous when they were offered a show to fix up houses on television!

Because Jonathan and Drew listened to their father and did not let anyone tell them they were too young, they discovered how many different skills they had at a young age.

You don't have to have a show to be a successful tradesman, although this is a great place to learn more about this skill. There are many shows on television about "flipping" houses (making them better). Ask your parents to help you find one, and get a firsthand look at what it is like to help make a home beautiful and how fun the work can be. Maybe you can offer to help your mom or dad paint a room or build shelves.

Dream of Creating Electric Robots

LIKE

Hannah Herbst

Look around at all the different things that use electricity: tablets, phones, microwaves, and many of the toys you play with. An electrical engineer designed all of these. Electrical engineers make sure the electrical parts in a product work together. Hannah Herbst is an electrical engineer who designed her first robot at the age of twelve, and by the age of fifteen, was presenting her idea to the President of the United States.

When she was young, Hannah's teachers told her that her math scores were not high enough to place in the advanced math or science classes. This made a future in math or science seem out of her reach, so she focused on other things she enjoyed, like art and theater. Her parents still believed in her abilities and made her leave her comfort zone to attend an engineering camp at the age of twelve.

Hannah arrived at camp on the first day, unsure of what to expect. She put on a bright pink theater t-shirt, smiled, and headed into the camp with her dad by her side. As she walked up to the camp, she began studying the other campers and realized that she was different from them. They were all boys.

She looked up at her dad with nervousness in her eyes and said, "Are you really going to leave me here with all these boys?"

Her father laughed, but made a deal with her, "If you stay and try this for one day and don't like it – you don't have to come back tomorrow."

Hannah agreed, thinking, "I will spend the next eight hours doing this in exchange for never having to do engineering ever again." The goal of the camp was to build a robot that would compete in a robot battle. The boys at the camp were happy to have her there – even showing her how to program and letting her do it herself. It was being included that made all the difference. Hannah saw that science was a hands-on process that demanded creativity to solve problems, and not a subject at school that she was told she was not smart enough for.

When Hannah looks back at her experience at camp she says, "To say this camp changed my life would be an understatement – I have been programming robots with boys ever since."

After she left camp, she joined every science group she could find, getting better and better at making robots. One day, her pen pal from Africa wrote to her, complaining that her town did not have electricity, which made life hard. Hannah saw this as a problem that her love of robots could help solve. Since she lived in Florida, she was always near the water. One day, while sitting by the ocean, Hannah thought that the movement of water could create energy to be harnessed and used by people like her friend. She worked on many different designs and finally created something that helped her friend in Africa get electricity. She was only thirteen years old.

Her design was submitted into a science competition and she won! Hannah was able to work with other electrical engineers on her idea. She was named America's best young scientist – all because she stepped outside of her comfort zone and was willing to be the only girl in engineering camp.

If you are interested in how electronics work and enjoy problem solving, Hannah says, "To all of you who have been told you are not smart enough for the smart class, or believe you can't build a robot because you have not been challenged to try – I challenge you to look around to find problems in the world around you and just start thinking about ways to solve them." You can find science fairs in your town or state and attend them, join a club, or find experiment books at your local library. There are many competitions to build robots and other things that require electricity.

43

Dream of Creating Futuristic Machines

LIKE

Elon Musk

Mechanical engineers are people who build machines. Think about all the machines that we use every day, like the cars we drive and the planes that fly. Someone had to think about all the moving parts and how they function together to work safely. One impressive man who has designed many different types of machines is Elon Musk. He has designed space rockets, cars that run on batteries, and a brand-new train system.

Elon is intelligent, with a strong imagination that helps him invent machines that did not exist before. Reading, especially science fiction, fueled his imagination and ability to dream of creating impossible things from a young age. Sometimes he would get lost in his books for almost ten hours per day. He would say that, "I was raised by books, books, and then my parents." One of his favorite book series was Isaac Asimov's *Foundation*, which is about the destruction and rebuilding of a universe in the future. Elon was already dreaming about the future of the world as a child. Sometimes, his dreams would enter his real life. When his parents were away, he built rockets in the backyard, dreaming of a future when he could fly off into space.

However, the other kids in his class did not understand him or his imagination. He was a small child and easy to pick on. One day, the kids in his class ganged up on him and pushed him down a flight of stairs, injuring him badly. During his recovery, he learned to rely on his hobbies to keep him busy and less lonely. By the age of twelve, he had designed his own video game, selling it for $500. He then joined up with his cousin to win a *Dungeons & Dragons* tournament. His cousin says that it was because of Elon's "incredible imagination" that they won.

It was this imagination that led him to ask himself in college, "What is the biggest issue that the world has to solve?" For Elon, it was our energy problem –we use too much gasoline and not enough power from sources that are easier to replace and less damaging to the earth. This is what made him decide to design the Tesla Car – a car that runs on a battery instead of gas. Today, you can see many of these cars on the road, all because of the engineering dream of one man.

His next dream was to help make space exploration easier. He wanted to give humans a chance at extended life on Mars. The greatest challenge was that rockets were so expensive; they cost billions of dollars to make, but we only use them once. Elon designed a reusable rocket that can be used more than once. His rocket was the first, outside of NASA, to deliver supplies to the international space station.

Today, Elon is working on a train that can be sent through a tube. This "train tube" would allow people to travel faster and without traffic, helping to save time, and just like his other ideas, save energy.

If building futuristic machines, like Elon, sounds fun to you – start by testing your technical skills with building kits. You can find them for all sorts of different models, like working cars, trucks, and airplanes. Lego makes a great kit set. However, don't forget that one of the things that makes great mechanical engineers special is their ability to imagine machines that don't exist yet, so don't just rely on kits- allow yourself to explore other possibilities, like going to a distant planet!

Dream of Creating Eco-Friendly Products

LIKE

Maya Penn

With all the new types of products that we are now capable of creating, there is one downside; all the trash that these new products create. Plastics and clothing are one of the biggest reasons that our dumps keep filling up. If you are dreaming about developing products, consider what Maya Penn is doing to help create products that are better for our planet.

Maya's journey started with her love of art. She was drawing as soon as she could hold a crayon. At the age of three, she would create flipbooks to simulate the cartoons that she saw on television. One day she was watching a show about career possibilities (sound familiar?), she learned that animation was a career and she decided to start practicing her cartoons immediately.

At the age of four she was learning how to use computers and came up with the idea for a cartoon about computer virus's that live inside of her computer. She created her first animation series and website. The more ideas she had, the better she became at making them come to life.

She would see ideas in everything around her, including old scraps of fabric around the house.

She would take these scraps of fabric and make hats, scarves and headbands. When she would wear her creations outside of her house, people would compliment her. They would say, "I love what you are wearing, where can I buy one of those?" She would reply, "from me!"

Her and her mom would sit on the front porch with all of their materials and create all sorts of designs. This motivated Maya to learn more about the fashion industry.

One of the things that she learned was the harm that clothing production can have on the environment. The dyes from the fabrics can get in the air and make people sick or be dumped in the ground and be bad for the environment. As soon as she learned this, she declared, "If my generation wants to have a greener tomorrow, I have to do my part. All of my products will be echo-friendly and I will give some of the money I make to people who help the environment."

At eight years old, Maya started her own store on *Etsy*, a website that sells crafts that people make. She was selling enough of her accessories that they were being purchased by people all over the world.

She was featured in the news for her work to make a difference for her generation. She says, "It's not about getting it through our heads, it's about getting it through our hearts, because that is when movements are sparked." You can see her products at www.mayasideas.com.

If you love the idea of making products or want to know more about the impact it has on the environment, National Geographic has a great section of their website that is all about this topic. Visit www.nationalgeographic.com/environment to read articles and watch videos about human impact on the environment. It is up to the next generation of producers to keep our planet healthy.

Dream of Creating Buildings

LIKE

I.M. Pei

If you have ever been to New York City, you know that there are buildings everywhere, as far as the eye can see. Each one has its own personality and adds to the look and feel of the city skyline. Even in the town you live in, there are buildings that probably stick out as being unique and special. People called architects create these buildings.

It is easy to imagine I.M. as a young boy in Shanghai, China, a city that is even bigger than New York City. His city was growing so fast that on each of his birthdays, the city would look different than the year before. He liked to think that the city was growing alongside him.

Geometry, which is a very special type of math that studies shapes, did not feel like math to I.M., it felt like art. Think about cutting up hundreds of squares, triangles, circles, and rectangles into pieces. The different ways that you put these shapes together is art. Designing them so that they become a building requires science. To I.M., architecture is both an art and a science.

I.M. was excited to figure out all the ways he could use shapes and geometry to create buildings like the ones he loved growing up. He left China to study architecture in America, but did not leave his love of China or the world behind. As I.M. began designing buildings, he would say, "I don't want my buildings all in one place, I want them all over the world. I want to learn all about new places." One of these places was France.

One of the most famous structures in all of France is not even a building – it is an entrance! When the president of France requested I.M. to reconstruct the Louvre, one of the most famous art museums in the world, I.M. realized that the worst problem the building had was that the front entrance was very crowded.

He took his love of shapes, light, and geometry and built a brand-new entrance in the shape of a huge glass pyramid right in the middle of the museum. When the structure was first built, many French people were upset because the new entrance did not match the design of the rest of the museum and was built by a Chinese American, not a French architect. The newspapers ran negative stories about I.M. However, I.M. stood by his design, proud of how the light and shape of the pyramid created its own art and beauty.

To be unique means to invite criticism from those who may not agree with you. If you want to design buildings that stand alone, sometimes the person who designs them must stand-alone as well.

Today, the Louvre is one of the most recognized buildings in not only France, but in the world. I.M. was an architect until he was 102 years old and designed many other famous buildings around the world – each reflecting his unique love of shapes and geometry.

If you are fascinated by buildings the way that I.M. was, there is no better toy than LEGOs to create structures and entire cities – simply from your imagination. If you are feeling super ambitious, there are LEGO sets that are specifically for kids interested in architecture, with thousands of pieces and instructions on how to replicate some of the most famous buildings in the world (Lego Studio – Architecture). Observe how buildings make you feel and research the origins of their designs.

23

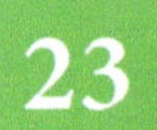

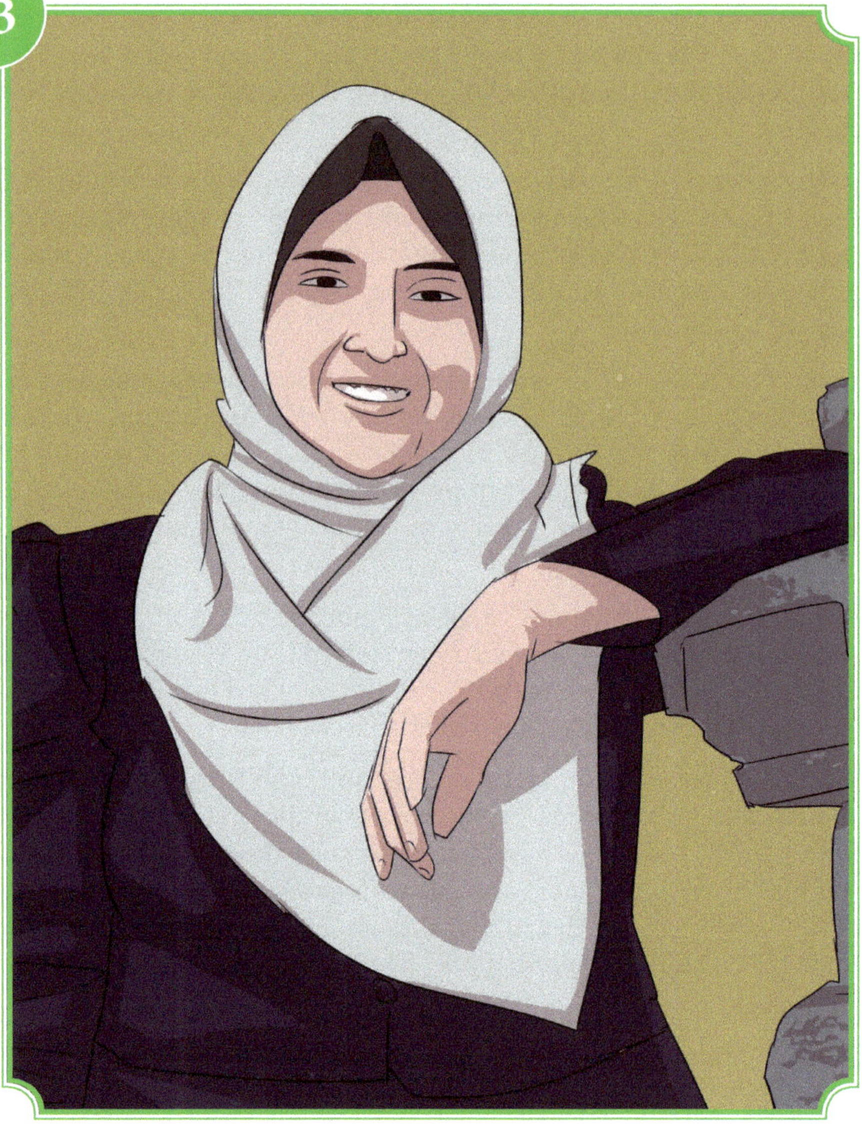

Dream of Creating Materials

LIKE

Majd Mashharawi

Every single item we use in daily life is made from a material developed and tested by someone. These people are material engineers. An engineer who figured out how to combine wax, charcoal, and chalk together invented the crayons that you color with. Astronauts need material engineers to create tools light enough for space travel.

Twenty Three-year-old Majd Mashharawi figured out how to use the rubble and ash in her war-torn neighborhood to create lighter, stronger, and cheaper bricks for her community to rebuild with.

Majd lives in a place called the Gaza Strip, which has been a source of religious conflict for many years. This conflict has caused thousands of homes to be destroyed, but most of them are unable to be rebuilt because they are made from cement, which is hard to get in Gaza.

Majd studied engineering in college and her program was only 1% female. People said she would not find a job because she was a woman, so she had to make a job for herself.

After graduation, Majd was standing in the hot sun, daydreaming about the future. As her eyes wandered to the neighbors and homes around her, she realized that there was an engineering problem to solve – right in front of her face.

How could she help families reclaim their destroyed homes? In Gaza, homes are passed down through generations and families rarely move, so rebuilding was about more than money. It was about pride and history.

What makes material engineers special is that they understand what materials are made of.

As Majd looked around her and saw the excess ash and rubble, she understood that ash had bonding properties, which in theory should take the place of some of the ingredients in normal cement.

She gathered the materials she needed and got to work. It took her 150 failed experiments and six months, but she figured out how to make building blocks out of the waste material in her own backyard.

To Majd, these are not just blocks.

"They are a change to the stereotype about women in Gaza. Most think that this is the type of work for men. We do can do lots of things if we are given the opportunity to do them. Education is the strongest weapon we have to fight for our freedom and future. We are not victims."

If you are interested in creating material on your own, a fun place to start is to make your own slime. There are lots of recipes on the internet. It is fun to see how a little glue, glitter, food coloring, baking soda, and contact solution will transform everyday items into something brand new.

Dream of Creating Video Games

LIKE

Ed McMillen and Tommy Refenes

When you turn on your computer or tablet, the programs make it fun. There are lots of different types of programs, like social media, television, shopping, photography, travel, health, cooking, and the list continues. People who make these programs are called software developers.

Ed and Tommy develop video games. Video game developers can work in large teams for big companies like Nintendo, or they can work independently, like Ed and Tommy, to develop their own games and sell them online. Ed and Tommy like developing games on their own because they get to do whatever they want, as they don't have any bosses to answer to, so their creativity is unlimited.

Ed grew up in California, on the beach. However, he did not spend his days making sandcastles, he spent it making monsters. He loved to draw and play video games, spending his days imagining different types of monsters. His teachers thought this was a problem, but his grandmother supported his creativity, telling him, "I know you will use this talent to be a success."

Creating video games on your own is very personal; your own life often ends up as part of the game. One of Ed's first games was about a monster that was isolated from other monsters and tried to go to other planets to make new friends. Each planet represented problems and insecurities that he had as a child.

Tommy was obsessed with video games from a very young age – every square inch of his bedroom was covered in video game posters and figurines. He pushed himself to play all the hardest games. His parents supported his love of video games and he began programming at the age of eleven. He spent his early career studying and learning at bigger companies until the age of twenty-five, when he started launching games of his own. Similar to Ed, he believes that "I can make something as a way to express myself."

Together, Ed and Tommy created a game called *Super Meat Boy*.

Their goal was to create a video game that the thirteen-year-old versions of themselves would love; a game that kids on the playground would argue and talk about. Ed used his love of drawing monsters to lead all the artwork and level design, while Tommy did all the coding (which is making the program work).

The game is about a boy monster whose girlfriend is kidnapped, so he must rescue her. The game has over three hundred levels but was designed to be fun and challenging, not frustrating. If Meat Boy dies, he has an infinite number of lives to come back and try again.

Super Meat Boy has sold over a million copies and was voted GameSpot's best downloadable console game in 2010. Tommy said that he is glad the game did so well, but more than success, he is glad that he made something he is truly proud of. Ed hopes that he inspired a kid like him to stay up all night, waiting for a new release and to spend the entire next day playing. "I hope I can inspire even just one kid like me to follow their creativity."

Coding is likely to be one of the most promising and exciting careers for your generation, whether it is on video games or other inventions that don't exist yet. It may seem complicated, but it is actually very easy to learn simple coding, and little by little, you can work up to making your own program. Remember, Tommy was eleven years old when he started. There are a lot of toys that teach coding. The Wonder Workshop (www.makewonder.com) is a great place to get started.

25

Dream of Creating Roller Coasters

LIKE

Michael Reitz

When a roller coaster does a loop-de-loop, do you ever wonder how you are able to stay in your seat and not fall out? When you go down a hill and you feel a drop in your stomach, you feel like you might fly out of your seat, but you don't. Understanding how a roller coaster car can create a thrill and still keep you safe is what a roller coaster engineer like Michal Reitz does.

When Michael was young, he was good at math and science and loved doing puzzles, so his parents encouraged him to become an engineer. He left the country to use his skills, including speaking German. When he came back to America, he thought maybe he would try and be a doctor instead. While he was waiting to start medical school, he saw an ad looking for a German-speaking engineer. Not knowing what the job was, he applied. He got a call asking if he would like to come and build roller coasters. Michael never went to medical school.

In fact, Michael is responsible for building *Kingda Ka* at Six Flags in Ocean County, New Jersey. *Kingda Ka* is the fastest roller coaster in America and the tallest in the world. In fact, it is twice as tall as the Statue of Liberty.

When you board a typical roller coaster, the ride starts off slowly as you climb the first hill. *Clink. Clink. Clink.* The car is pulled up the first hill by a chain. Then, as you hit the top, gravity takes over as you roll over the top and rush down the first hill and backup the next hill until the ride is over.

When Michael was dreaming of how to make his new roller coaster bigger and better, he thought, what if you didn't have to wait for the thrill? He studied what Air Force pilots were capable of. F-18's, some of the fastest planes on the planet, are used in far off countries and often have to take off and land on a runway built on the top of a ship! This means that they have to take off and land fast. What if a roller coaster could use this same technology to take off like a fighter plane?

Michael discovered how to make a roller coaster that acts like a slingshot. Using a scientific technology called hydraulics, the ride could go up to 128 miles per hour in three seconds! With all that speed, the train shot straight up one side of a U-shaped track and then whooshed down the other side. The whole ride was over in one minute. It took a deep understanding of physics, a type of science, to make sure that the ride was made safely.

Michael says that his job is to calculate the forces that riders will experience and stay safely in their seats. "I believe that we love controlled fear. We want to be afraid and push ourselves to the limit. But we also want to know that we are safe."

Michael loves working at an amusement park because he gets to be one of the first people to try out a new ride. He also gets to watch the reaction of other people experiencing the ride for the first time. "I love watching people come off the ride laughing and screaming," he says.

If you are interested in building structures that can provide transport, travel, or a thrill, Michael says, "You must have a strong understanding of science and math. Practice your engineering skills by building and taking things apart!" There are also "Discovering STEM" toys focused on building structures, where you can start learning some of the core principles that allow a roller coaster to be shot like a slingshot through the air and back in under a minute!

Dream of Creating Food

LIKE

Kwame Onwuachi

When you get older, the foods that you eat today will always make you think of home. Maybe it is a gooey grilled cheese or a homemade pizza straight from the oven. For Kwame Onwuachi, the foods that he grew up learning to eat and to cook would forever shape his life as a chef.

When Kwame was growing up, trouble seemed to find him. He was often in trouble at school, though he was a good kid who wanted to do better. Cooking gave him focus and purpose, and by the age of twenty-six, he was running his own restaurant. His restaurant became famous because it had thirteen courses of food, each representing a story from his life.

His menu and story started in the kitchen with his mother, who was a professional caterer. They would stand side by side at the counter and peel shrimp and make gumbo together. For Kwame, there were no greater moments of love between him and his mother than when they were preparing a meal together.

His grandfather also played a role in contributing to the "menu of his life." At the age of twelve, Kwame went to live with him in Africa, where he learned to appreciate Nigerian food. This type of food required a different level of work and creativity because he didn't have the tools he was used to from his mother's kitchen. These foods would make up another set of dishes in his thirteen-course menu.

Kwame really learned to love cooking in the most unexpected of places: an oil drilling platform in the middle of the ocean. It was there he learned that cooking could tell a story. He spent his spare time socializing with the crew and listening to their stories of home.

Without access to the internet to look up recipes, he would only have these stories to work from. Still, he created special meals for the men that reminded them of home. He started out as the assistant cook, but quickly replaced the main cook because of how much everyone loved his menus.

Once Kwame understood that cooking wasn't just food, it was an experience, he decided he wanted to own his own catering company.

He moved to New York and sold candy on the subway to raise money to start his company. This too, would end up influencing his thirteen-course menu. His very first job was for almost two thousand people and all he had was a chef coat and a business card. Without letting on that he didn't really have a business, he managed to get a kitchen, a staff, and the food he needed in only a matter of weeks!

From there, his luck grew and grew. He would go on to study at a top-rated cooking school, work at one of the finest restaurants in New York, and compete on *Top Chef*. However, after being told by someone that "America wasn't ready for a Black chef that made fancy meals," he knew that it was time to tell his story via food. He was able to find someone who believed in his idea and helped him open his own restaurant. He laid out a menu that was a reflection of his life and would tell his story as he served each course.

Just like Kwame did with his mother, for the men on the oilrig, and for the people in his restaurant, cooking is a wonderful way to show your family that you love them. There are YouTube videos (The Bow Girls), Kits (Radish Kids), and TV shows (Top Chef Junior) all meant to teach and inspire young people to become budding chefs.

Dream of Creating Baked Goods

LIKE

Jasmine Cho

The difference between cakes, cupcakes, muffins, and cookies is a subtle one. They use a lot of the same ingredients, but how much of each and at what temperature determines if the final product is fluffy like a cupcake or dense like a muffin. This is why baking is often seen as more of a "science" than the art of cooking.

However, Jasmine Cho is proof that baking is also an art. She uses cookies to help tell the stories of Asian American history.

When Jasmine was in elementary school she was bullied and teased because of her Asian heritage. These experiences stuck with her as she became an adult. She can recall a time when her feelings were hurt because someone assumed that she could not speak English simply because of how she looked. When she was working at a school in a diverse neighborhood, one of the children greeted her with excitement and he asked her where she was from. She told him, "I am from America, my parents are from South Korea - do you know where that is?" After pausing, the boy responded by asking another question, "Is this your translator?" This was a confusing moment for Jasmine, having just answered his question in English. It made her feel that she wasn't being seen, even standing right in front of this boy and having grown up in this country.

This feeling was reinforced in college when she took a course in Asian American history. There were so many Asian Americans that should have been in history books, but she had never heard of them.

She had just started her own bakery and she knew then, in her heart, what she needed to put on her edible canvases (her cookies): the faces of those who were not being remembered in other ways.

Jasmine says, "Privilege is when your history is taught as core curriculum while mine is taught as an elective."

One person she decided to honor with her cookie art was Sammy Lee. He was the first Asian American to win a gold medal in swimming for the United States. However, because it was 1930, he wasn't allowed to swim in the same pool as other people because he was seen as different. He had to practice in a sand pit in his backyard.

You can't eat all of her works of art, as some cookies she covers in glue and saves. However, her artistic cookies have received news attention around the world and have helped shine a light on these Asian American heroes. Jasmine says, "Anything can be done with a little sugar, flour, and imagination!"

What could you make with sugar, flour, and imagination? One great way to learn about baking is to have a baking day with your favorite baker, maybe your father or a grandmother?

Choose four different recipes and learn about what makes the ingredients behave differently. Cakes, cupcakes, cookies, and muffins – pay attention to what recipes require more or less of different ingredients and learn the science behind what those ingredients do. This basic lesson will help you bake lots of other things as well.

28

Dream of Creating Websites

LIKE

Jessica Mah

As of 2020, there are nearly two billion active websites on the internet. For each of these websites, someone had to have the idea, build it, and make it work. This is called website programming. While this can take time to learn, this skill is accessible to anyone in the world, of any age, that has an internet connection. Jessica Mah was in middle school when she started programming and using this skill to make money.

Jessica learned to program by going to the library and checking out books on website programming. She would sit for hours, reading and practicing what she learned. Being able to create something unique fascinated her. It wasn't until her mom, who owned her own company, asked her, "Why don't you take your programming skills and make a company out of it?" that she decided programming could be more than a hobby. Before she was even able to drive, Jessica was making money selling her programming services to other people.

Jessica enjoyed providing this service so much that she went on to study computer science in college.

She met a friend named Andrew Su in one of her classes and they studied together. One day, they finished their studies early and Andrew suggested that they do something fun together. For them, fun was working on programming projects. So, they got together and started coming up with ideas for programs that they could build.

Jessica thought back to her first business, remembering how difficult it was to track the money coming in and out. There were services that helped big companies to manage this, but nothing for little companies that were simple and easy to use. Andrew thought this was a great idea as well, so they started designing a program to help solve this problem. From there InDinero was born.

Similar to Jessica's story, lots of other websites started off as ideas in a dorm room. Facebook was once just a silly idea that a bunch of friends put together as a joke. Snapchat was the result of two college students sending a silly photo and wishing they could take it back. Jessica says, "You shouldn't wait until college to try something or learn something – just go out and try it!"

After graduation, that is exactly what she did. She started building her idea and was invited into a program that helped young companies get their start. The people running the program loved her idea so much that she left the program with over a million dollars to finish building her website.

Today, her website is thriving, and she is grateful that she discovered a hobby at a young age that would turn into a career she loved.

Like Jessica, you don't have to wait to go to college to learn how to create your own website. There are lots of free programs like CodeDragon and CodeaKid that teach web programming to kids through easy and fun games.

Wouldn't it be fun to build a website about your family or your favorite hobby that you could show off to your friends? If you are artistic, like to bake, or know how to make something cool, you could create a website and start your own small business.

29

Dream of Creating Flight

LIKE

Richard Browning

One of the things that people relate to "the future" is when humans can figure out how to fly. Well, the future might be closer than people think. Richard Browning is a modern day Iron Man who is building a jet suit that is already breaking world records for human flight.

Richard's whole family loved flight.

His father was an aeronautical engineer and independent thinker who was fascinated by the idea of human flight. He even had a bike with wings on it! One grandfather ran a helicopter company. Another grandfather was a wartime pilot. So, it was no surprise when Richard started tinkering with small jet engines in his spare time, figuring out if they could be used for human flight.

First, he attached one to each arm; he could jump up and down and catch some air. So, he thought, "Well, there is only one sensible next step – get two more." He put two on his arms and two on his legs. It didn't work. He knew that the whole journey was about trying lots of things and failing most of the time.

Finally, his first coherent flight lasted six seconds. He kept refining it. He also kept falling over.

Richard says, "I tried a lot of hard things, like getting my green beret (in the army) that gave me the confidence to ask 'what if', and then go and try it. Four out of five times, I would fail, but one of those times I wouldn't, and it would make the failures worth it.

If you looked at the problem on paper, you could come up with all of the reasons it shouldn't work. For example, some would say that the sheer force would make the engines whip around like a fire hose. They would stop there and say, it's not worth trying. Well, trying taught us that it could work."

It took three years, but those original experiments turned into three fully-functional jet suits.

Richard doesn't know when and how everyday people will use this technology, but he is hopeful. For now, his plan is to run flight races. People have a fascination with watching people fly. He says, "NASCAR and Formula One are vehicles that are not very practical at all, but are wildly entertaining, inspire, and push our understanding of technology. We can do the same with jet suits."

His plan is to build a race series where up to six pilots race up to fifty miles per hour over water. The races will happen in interesting places all over the world.

Richard hopes that putting this technology out in the world that it will inspire innovation that is better and faster than what they came up with and lead to more practical uses.

"I've flown hundreds of times and it is a rush each time," Richard says.

Richard also believes that your generation is the key to this next leap in technology. He says, "The future of aeronautical innovation rests on the shoulders of those we inspire today. My company is committed to demonstrating to young people and students across the globe that human flight is not just a possibility, but already a reality." You can find easy to understand explanations of how this technology works on the STEM section of his website - https://gravity.co/stem/.

30

Dream of Creating Motorcycles

LIKE

Paul Teutul Jr.

If you want to put two pieces of paper together when you are crafting, what do you do? You use glue to stick them together. When making things that have heavier materials than paper (like metal), you have to use heat to put the parts together. This process is called welding. Paul Teutul Jr. (just called Junior) is a welder who uses his skills to create custom motorcycles that are unlike any other motorcycles in the world.

When Junior was a kid, he didn't like reading books as much as he liked making things with his hands. He learned more by doing things than reading about them.

When he got a new toy, he would immediately look to see if it said "assembly required." His favorite part was putting the toy together. He could just look at the picture in the instructions and figure out how all the pieces could come together.

As a teenager, he began working as soon as he was able. His father owned an iron shop where Junior learned his welding skills at age thirteen. He worked harder and longer than most adults and was put in charge of making railings. Once he learned the skill, what really excited him was how creative he could be with it.

His father started a second business making motorcycles (a type called choppers) and asked for his son's help. This was when his creativity really started to shine.

The problem-solving skills he used to build his own toys helped him imagine creative new ways to build a motorcycle. He could see the motorcycle in his mind that he wanted to build and then figure out the steps to build it.

He wanted to do more than just assemble bikes. He wanted to make them different and works of art.

One of his first bikes he designed was called the "black widow". It was inspired by Spider-Man and had webs in the spokes, spider-thin frames, and a paint job to match. It even had eyes on either side of the gas tank.

He did this first bike as a side project, and when they took this chopper to a motorcycle show, people loved it. So, Junior kept coming up with unique themes, like a fighter jet, the Yankees baseball team, and a tribute to the fallen fire fighters of September 11th.

Eventually, the father/son motorcycles started becoming popular enough that someone decided to make a television show about them. A TV crew would follow them around and film them designing and welding their bikes. People loved watching this type of creativity so much that even if they were not motorcycle fans or didn't know anything about welding, they were still big fans of the show.

The show was so popular that it lasted over ten years. It helped make people aware of what a creative job welding can be.

Welding is used in lots of industries and is a job that needs more people. If you are interested in welding, you might be able to find "trade classes" offered through your high school. There are also welding camps around the country where you can learn to weld as early as age twelve.

31

Dream of Creating New Foods

LIKE

Alton Brown

Frosted Flakes, Kraft Macaroni and Cheese, and Bomb Pop Popsicles are not foods that come straight from nature. These products are made in a food laboratory. The people who invent these foods are called food scientists. The way that food reacts to heat and cold, the ingredients required to make a new recipe come out correctly, and the understanding of food nutrition all require a chemical understanding of foods. Alton

Brown is a food scientist that creates new foods on his show *Good Eats*. On his show he helps explain to people the science behind the food he is making.

Alton started making food with his mother and grandmother at an early age and began developing his skills. When he was growing up, he can remember standing at the griddle waiting for pancakes to bubble up and be ready to flip over. "Pancakes were more than a food.

They were a culinary right of passage. They were often the first dish that us kids learned how to make," Alton says remembering how he learned to cook.

Later, he would use these skills in college to impress girls. In college he studied theater and his parents would joke, "the only thing a theater degree will get you is a job in a restaurant." Even though it's not what they meant, they ended up being right.

He used his theater degree to work in cinema, specifically making commercials, but he was more interested in watching cooking shows and thought, "This would be a lot more fun to work on than commercials." One day he stopped what he was doing and wrote down what his dream cooking show would be like. He wrote down the name of a famous chef (Julia Child), a scientist (Mr. Wizard) and a comedy (Monty Python). He said, "I want the show to be all three things: science, comedy and food. I want people to know what makes food tick, rather than simply being hit over the head with recipes. And hopefully they would be so entertained that they wouldn't know they were being educated."

He left his job and started at a culinary school, where you learn about cooking and the science behind it. He used his skills from making commercials to make several audition tapes and sent them to the Food Network TV channel. They loved his idea and hired him to make more. His show was so loved that he worked on it for over 10 years.

An example of one of his episodes was when he explained the science behind ice cream. Ice cream is just like candy making. Both things are about controlling sugar crystals, known as sucrose. What makes ice cream more complicated than making candy is that you also have to control ice crystals as well. The sucrose prevents the large ice crystals from forming and that is why ice cream can come out of the freezer creamy and smooth, unlike other things that come out hard as a block. Without understanding the chemistry of sugar and freezing water, we would not have ice cream. To make it even more interesting, there is a concept called "overrun" which determines the amount of air that is added to the sugar and water mixture. The more air, the fluffier the ice cream.

Alton has 3 great books called *Good Eats* that contain all the recipes from his shows that includes the science behind the method, similar to the ice cream example. You can also watch his *Good Eats* TV show on Food Network and Youtube. If you're interested in cooking and were thinking of being a chef, a food scientist is another career you may enjoy. Not only can you get the joy of inventing new foods, but you get to see them on the shelf at your grocery store.

DREAM IT & do it

100 POSSIBILITIES, STORIES, REAL-LIFE ROLE MODELS.

FOR GIRLS AND BOYS

INSPIRING ALL THE THINGS YOU CAN BE

HOLLY A. SHARP